How to Design
Survey Studies
2nd edition

THE SURVEY KIT, Second Edition

Purposes: The purposes of this 10-volume Kit are to enable readers to prepare and conduct surveys and to help readers become better users of survey results. Surveys are conducted to collect information; surveyors ask questions of people on the telephone, face-to-face, and by mail. The questions can be about attitudes, beliefs, and behavior as well as socioeconomic and health status. To do a good survey, one must know how to plan and budget for all survey tasks, how to ask questions, how to design the survey (research) project, how to sample respondents, how to collect reliable and valid information, and how to analyze and report the results.

Users: The Kit is for students in undergraduate and graduate classes in the social and health sciences and for individuals in the public and private sectors who are responsible for conducting and using surveys. Its primary goal is to enable users to prepare surveys and collect data that are accurate and useful for primarily practical purposes. Sometimes, these practical purposes overlap with the objectives of scientific research, and so survey researchers will also find the Kit useful.

Format of the Kit: All books in the series contain instructional objectives, exercises and answers, examples of surveys in use and illustrations of survey questions, guidelines for action, checklists of dos and don'ts, and annotated references.

Volumes in The Survey Kit:

1. **The Survey Handbook, 2nd**
   Arlene Fink
2. **How to Ask Survey Questions, 2nd**
   Arlene Fink
3. **How to Conduct Self-Administered and Mail Surveys, 2nd**
   Linda B. Bourque and Eve P. Fielder
4. **How to Conduct Telephone Surveys, 2nd**
   Linda B. Bourque and Eve P. Fielder
5. **How to Conduct In-Person Interviews for Surveys, 2nd**
   Sabine Mertens Oishi
6. **How to Design Survey Studies, 2nd**
   Arlene Fink
7. **How to Sample in Surveys, 2nd**
   Arlene Fink
8. **How to Assess and Interpret Survey Psychometrics, 2nd**
   Mark S. Litwin
9. **How to Manage, Analyze, and Interpret Survey Data, 2nd**
   Arlene Fink
10. **How to Report on Surveys, 2nd**
    Arlene Fink

Arlene Fink

How to Design Survey Studies
2nd edition

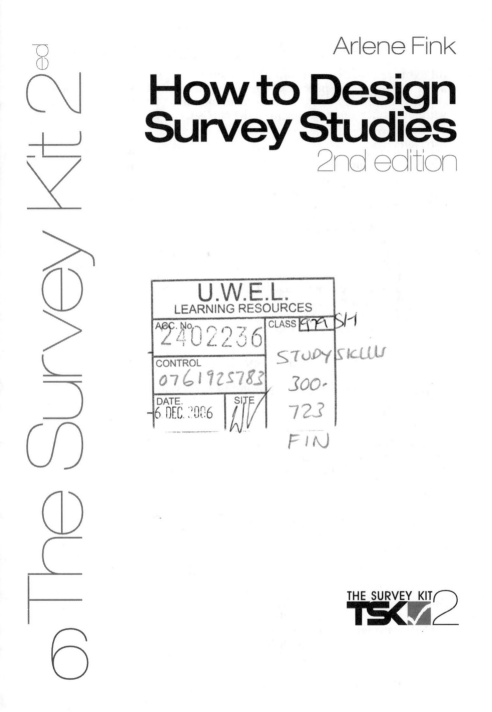

THE SURVEY KIT 2

TSK 2

The Survey Kit 2 ed

6

SAGE Publications
International Educational and Professional Publisher
Thousand Oaks ■ London ■ New Delhi

For information:

 Sage Publications, Inc.
2455 Teller Road
Thousand Oaks, California 91320
E-mail: order@sagepub.com

Sage Publications Ltd.
6 Bonhill Street
London EC2A 4PU
United Kingdom

Sage Publications India Pvt. Ltd.
M-32 Market
Greater Kailash I
New Delhi 110 048 India

Printed in the United States of America

Library of Congress Cataloging-in-Publication Data

The survey kit.—2nd ed.
    p. cm.
Includes bibliographical references.
ISBN 0-7619-2510-4 (set : pbk.)
1. Social surveys. 2. Health surveys. I. Fink, Arlene.
HN29 .S724 2002
300'.723—dc21   2002012405

This book is printed on acid-free paper.

02 03 04 05 10 9 8 7 6 5 4 3 2 1

Acquisitions Editor:	C. Deborah Laughton
Editorial Assistant:	Veronica Novak
Copy Editor:	Judy Selhorst
Production Editor:	Diane S. Foster
Typesetter:	Bramble Books
Proofreader:	Cheryl Rivard
Cover Designer:	Ravi Balasuriya
Production Designer:	Michelle Lee

Contents

How to Design Survey Studies: Learning Objectives

The aim of this book is to guide you in selecting and using appropriate survey designs. The specific objectives are as follows:

- Describe the major features of high-quality survey systems
- Identify the questions that structure survey designs
- Distinguish between experimental and observational designs
- Explain the characteristics, benefits, and concerns of these designs:

  - Concurrent controls with random assignment

  - Concurrent controls without random assignment

  - Self-controls

  - Historical controls

  - Solomon four-group designs

  - Descriptive and experimental factorial designs

  - Cross-sectional designs

  - Cohort designs

  - Case-control designs

- Identify the risks to a design's internal validity
- Identify the risks to a design's external validity

1 Useful Surveys

Surveys are systems for collecting information from or about people to describe, compare, or explain their knowledge, attitudes, and behavior. They are used to collect data on a broad range of subjects of interest in fields as diverse as education, sociology, demography, health, psychology, economics, business, and law. The best survey information systems have these six features:

- Specific, measurable objectives
- Sound research design
- Sound choice of population or sample
- Reliable and valid instruments
- Appropriate analysis
- Accurate reporting of results

Features of Well-Designed Survey Studies

MEASURABLE OBJECTIVES

A survey's objectives are considered to be **measurable** if two or more people can easily agree on all the words and terms used to describe the survey's purposes. Example 1.1 provides samples of some measurable survey objectives.

EXAMPLE 1.1
Three Measurable Objectives

Objective 1: To determine the quality of UCLA's education in preparing students with important job-related skills. Quality is a combination of the skill's importance and the value of UCLA's education in teaching the skill.

> *Comment:* This objective becomes measurable when the term *quality* is clearly defined to mean importance and value. You can infer that some of the survey's questions will take forms like "Select the top three most important skills" and "Rate how valuable UCLA's education is, using a scale on which 1 = *not very valuable,* 3 = *medium value,* and 5 = *extremely valuable.*"

Objective 2: To determine changes from 1994 to 2002 qualifications, such as advanced placement units, among entering students.

> *Comment:* Qualifications are made measurable by "advanced placement units."

Objective 3: To compare the effectiveness of three approaches to continuing mental health education in a workshop setting. The three approaches are (a) traditional lecture and small group discussion, (b) computerized cases and small group discussion, and (c) computerized cases and self-instruction. An effective approach is one that encourages participants to resolve important (as defined by experts) patient care issues in practice appropriately.

Comment: An *effective approach* is defined as one that encourages workshop participants to resolve important patient care issues appropriately.

SOUND RESEARCH DESIGN

The term **design** in this context refers to the surveyor's way of arranging the environment in which a survey takes place. The environment consists of the individuals or groups of people, places, activities, or objects that are to be surveyed.

Some designs are relatively simple. A fairly uncomplicated survey might consist of a 10-minute interview on Wednesday with a group of 50 children to find out if they enjoyed a given film and, if so, why. Because such a survey would provide a cross-sectional portrait of one group's opinions at a particular time, this kind of design is called **cross-sectional.**

More complicated survey designs use environmental arrangements that are experiments, relying on two or more groups of participants or observations. When a surveyor compares the views of randomly constituted groups of 50 children each, for example, the survey design is **experimental.**

SOUND SAMPLING

The participants in a survey may consist of all members of a given group or population, such as all 500 students in a school or all 70 patients at a particular health center who in the past 6 months have been diagnosed with diabetes. A subset of the population—say, 100 students or 25 patients—is a *sample*. In an ideal sample, the characteristics of the individuals who make up the sample are distributed in the same proportions as they are in the entire population of which the sample is a part. For example, an ideal sample would have the same proportion of males and females as is found in the larger population. To get a **representative sample**, a surveyor must use an unbiased method to choose survey participants and obtain adequate numbers of participants.

RELIABLE AND VALID INSTRUMENTS

A **reliable** survey instrument is one that gets consistent results; a **valid** one obtains accurate results. Traditionally, survey instruments have been equated with mailed or self-administered questionnaires and the instruments used by interviewers conducting telephone or in-person interviews. But the techniques for collecting and recording reliable and valid information perfected by survey researchers for these instruments have also been applied to other information-gathering techniques. These include forms used to conduct surveys regarding the quality of medical care, the use of financial resources, and the content of the professional literature in business, health, and education.

One indication of the adaptation of these survey techniques to other instruments is the similarity of their purposes: to describe, compare, and predict. Another indication is how similar a questionnaire or interview form is in content to, say, a record review form, which "asks" questions of records rather than of people. As the following examples illustrate, the two types of forms are practically identical:

Question from a self-administered questionnaire:

Which best describes your personal income last year? Circle *one* choice only.	
$25,000 or less	1
$25,001-$40,000	2
$40,001-$75,000	3
$75,001 or more	4

Question from a form for reviewing financial records:

Which best describes this person's income last year? Circle *one* choice only.	
$25,000 or less	1
$25,001-$40,000	2
$40,001-$75,000	3
$75,001 or more	4

All survey instruments, regardless of format, should contain only questions or items that are pertinent to the survey's objectives. The aim of any survey is to produce reliable and valid data. Reliable data come from consistent responses over time and between and among observers and respondents. Valid data come from surveys that measure what they purport to measure.

APPROPRIATE ANALYSIS

Surveyors use conventional statistical and other scholarly methods to analyze their findings. The choice of method depends on both the size of the sample and whether the surveyor's purpose is description, comparison, association (or correlation), or prediction. The analysis must also account for the type of survey data available: nominal (categorical), ordinal, or numerical. Nominal or categorical data come from scales that have no numerical value, such as gender and race. Ordinal data come from rating scales and may range, say, from *most favored* to *least favored,* or from *strongly agree* to *strongly disagree.* Numerical data come from measures that ask for numbers, such as age, years living at present address, and height.

ACCURATE REPORTING

To report survey results fairly and accurately, surveyors must stay within the boundaries set by the survey design, sampling methods, data collection quality, and choice of analysis. They must also be knowledgeable regarding the numerous ways tables and figures can be used to present information.

Survey Design: The Arranged Environment

To be useful and valid, a survey should be conducted in an arranged or designed environment. Consider the illustrations offered in Example 1.2. The aim of Survey 1 in the example is to find out if UCLA has done a good job in preparing its students with important job-related skills. This cross-sectional survey design provides a one-time-only portrait of students' opinions as gathered from a self-administered questionnaire (cross-sectional design is discussed in much greater detail in Chapter 2). Survey 2 collects data from records in two cross-sectional studies.

Survey 3 in Example 1.2 uses an experimental design to compare the results of observations and self-administered questionnaires. Experimental designs involve arranging the environment so that comparisons can be made. A relatively simple experimental design, for example, would compare the reading ability of children who have participated in an innovative program with the reading ability of children who have not participated. Survey 4 in the example also uses an experimental design, but in this case the three groups have been randomly assembled. Surveys 3 and 4 both use self-administered questionnaires. Survey 3 also uses observations, and Survey 4 also uses record reviews.

EXAMPLE 1.2
Illustrative Survey Designs

Survey 1: College Students and Graduates

Background: Each year, UCLA prepares a student profile. Data for the profile come from records (including those maintained by the Financial Aid Office and Student Loan Services) and mailed student questionnaires.

Objective: To determine the quality of UCLA's education in preparing students with important job-related skills

Instrument: Self-administered questionnaire. Students were asked to indicate on a 3-point scale how important each of eight items was in preparing them for their jobs and then to rate on a 4-point scale the quality of UCLA's preparation in each of the eight areas.

Design: Descriptive (or observational); specifically, cross-sectional

Results: The responses for graduates who were employed full-time and not enrolled in graduate school are summarized in Figure 1.1.

Example 1.2 continued

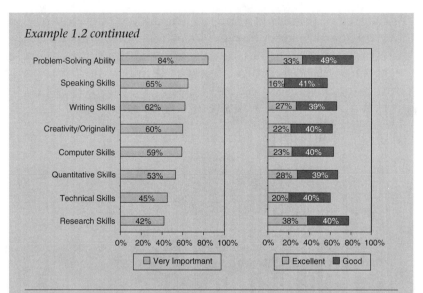

Figure 1.1.   UCLA Preparation

NOTE: Students were asked to indicate on a 3-point scale how important each of the eight items was in preparing them for their jobs and then to rate on a 4-point scale the quality of UCLA's preparation in each of the eight areas. The responses for graduates who were employed full-time and not enrolled in graduate school are summarized in this figure. *Problem-solving ability* was the area most often considered by respondents to be very important for the work they were currently doing, and it also received the highest combined rating of excellent or good. *Speaking skills* were second in terms of those who considered this area very important for their job, but last in the combined rating of excellent or good.

Interpretation: Problem-solving ability was the area most respondents considered to be very important for the work they were currently doing, and it also received the highest combined rating of excellent or good. Speaking skills were second in terms of those who considered them very important for their jobs, but last in the combined rating of excellent or good.

Comment: This survey provides a cross section of descriptive information at one point in time. The survey collected information directly from students through a self-administered questionnaire.

Example 1.2 continued

Survey 2: Entering Students

Background: As part of its annual student profile, UCLA collects data on students who enter with advanced placement (AP) units.

Objective: To assess the extent of change in the proportion of students entering UCLA with AP credits

Instrument: Standardized record review (records from Undergraduate Admissions and Relations With Schools)

Design: Cross-sectional (to study trends)

Results: Figure 1.2 shows the percentages of entering students with AP credits in 1994 and 2002.

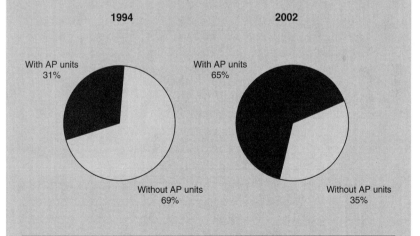

Figure 1.2. First-Year Students Enter With One Quarter's College Credit

NOTE: The percentage of students entering with AP units has continued to increase from 31% in 1994 to 65% in 2002, and the average amount of college credit earned increased from 14 to 18 units.

Example 1.2 continued

Interpretation: The percentage of students entering with AP units increased from 31% in 1994 to 65% in 2002. The average amount of college credit earned increased from 14 to 18 units.

Comment: This survey provides a description of trends in accumulating AP credits of two entering classes. Data came from a survey of records, using the same form each time.

Survey 3: Comparing Educational Approaches

Background: The city is conducting a study to identify an effective approach to continuing education in mental health.

Purpose: To compare the effectiveness of three approaches to instruction in a workshop setting

Instrument: Self-administered questionnaires and standardized 10-item observation form used by two trained observers monitoring each workshop

Design: An experiment with concurrent controls in which survey participants are not randomly assigned to groups. Here, 200 eligible community mental health workers were assigned to three workshops, depending on their preference. The first workshop (Group 1) used traditional lecture and small group discussion, the second (Group 2) relied on computerized cases and small group discussion, and the third (Group 3) employed computerized cases and self-instruction. Observations were made during each workshop session. Participants completed a questionnaire at the conclusion of the 3-hour workshop.

Example 1.2 continued

Results: Agreement between the two observers in each workshop was 81%, 76%, and 93% in Groups 1, 2, and 3, respectively. No differences were found in preferences for type of instruction among participants in the three groups. Participants in the computerized cases and self-instruction group (Group 3) rated their experiences as "likely to carry over into their work" significantly more often than did participants in the other two groups ($p < .05.$).

Interpretation: Participants in the computerized cases and self-instruction group stated that their learning is likely to carry over to their jobs significantly more often than did participants in the other groups. Their belief should now be tested in a controlled study.

Comment: This experimental study used a traditional survey method (a self-administered questionnaire) and an applied survey method (standardized observation) to collect data. Each type of survey information was collected just once: during the workshop (the observations) and at the conclusion of workshop participation (the questionnaire).

Survey 4: Comparing Educational Approaches

Background: The city is conducting a study to identify an effective approach to continuing education in mental health.

Purpose: To compare the effectiveness of three approaches to instruction by determining the number of important issues per topic (e.g., technical care, doctor-patient relationship, coordination of care) addressed in practice by participants. Important issues in patient care have been identified by a panel of experts.

Example 1.2 continued

Instrument: Self-administered questionnaires and case record review

Design: An experiment with concurrent controls in which survey participants are randomly assigned to groups. Here, 200 eligible community mental health workers were assigned at random to three workshops. The first workshop (Group 1) used traditional lecture and small group discussion, the second (Group 2) relied on computerized cases and small group discussion, and the third (Group 3) employed computerized cases and self-instruction. Participants completed a questionnaire at the conclusion of the 3-hour workshop. Before the workshops and 6 months after, the survey team reviewed the case records of participants and counted the number of important issues addressed.

Results: The number of issues (e.g., improving the doctor-patient relationship, fostering patient responsibility) addressed did not differ among the groups at baseline but differed significantly after the intervention. The number dropped significantly in Group 1 (2 to 0.5, $p < .05$); rose, but not significantly, in Group 2 (0.5 to 1.5, *ns* [not significant]), and increased substantially and significantly in Group 3 (1 to 3.75, $p < .05$). (For more information on testing statistical significance and p values, see **How to Manage, Analyze, and Interpret Survey Data**, Volume 9 in this series.) These results are shown in Figure 1.3.

Example 1.2 continued

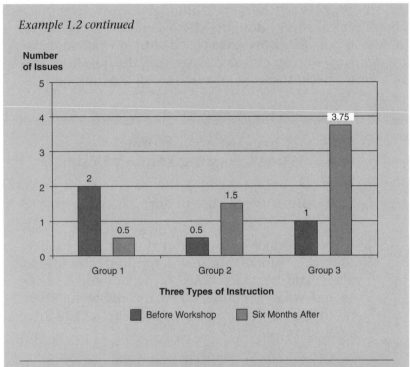

Figure 1.3.   Number of Issues per Topic Before and After Workshop

When Group 3 participants were asked to rate the likelihood that participation in the workshop contributed to their knowledge of important issues in caring for patients' mental health needs, nearly all (98%) chose ratings of 4 ("probably") or 5 ("definitely likely").

Interpretation: The use of computerized cases and self-instruction is an effective approach to continuing education for the city's mental health workers.

Comment: This study was experimental, and participants were randomly assigned to one of three groups. The survey team used questionnaires and record reviews to collect data.

The four surveys serving as illustrations in Example 1.2 all use typical survey designs. These can be grouped into two general types: *descriptive* (also called *observational*) and *experimental*. How do you choose? Answering the questions in the following checklist can help you to select the right design.

Checklist of Questions to Ask When Choosing a Survey Design

✓ What is the survey's aim (to describe, compare, predict)?

Surveys produce information that can be used to describe, compare, and predict attitudes, opinions, values, and behavior based on what people say or see and what is contained in records about them and their activities. Example 1.3 illustrates the three major survey aims.

EXAMPLE 1.3
Describing, Comparing, and Predicting

Describing

Objective: To *describe* the quality of life of men over and under 65 years of age with different health characteristics (e.g., the presence or absence of common conditions such as hypertension and diabetes) and social characteristics (e.g., living alone or living with someone; employed or not), all of whom have had surgery within the past 2 years for prostate cancer

Target: Men of differing ages, health, and social characteristics who have had surgery for prostate cancer within the past 2 years

Example 1.3 continued

Number of times surveyed: Once, within 2 years of surgery

Comparing—Design 1

Objective: At the end of the school year, to *compare* a sample of boys and girls in grades 1 through 6 in five schools regarding their views on their school's new dress code

Target: Boys and girls in grades 1 through 6 in five elementary schools

Number of times surveyed: Once, at the end of the school year

Comparing—Design 2

Objective: To *compare*, before and after participation in a safety course, parents of children under 5 years of age, between 6 and 12, and 13 and over in terms of their opinions of their ability to cope with potential accidents and injuries in the home

Target: Parents who participate in a safety course

Number of times surveyed: Twice, before and after participation

Comparing—Design 3

Objective: To *compare* a sample of employees in three companies annually for 3 years about their views on uncompensated leave time

Target: Employees in three companies

Example 1.3 continued

Number of times surveyed: Three times, once each year

Predicting

Objective: To determine the extent to which gender, education, and income *predict* preferences for differing leisure activities, including reading, sports, movies, and travel, in 2001 and 2002

Target: Male and female high school graduates, each of whom earns an annual income of less than $30,000, between $30,000 and $60,000, or more than $60,000

Number of times surveyed: Twice, in 2001 and in 2002

✓ Is a control group included?

A **group** is an assembly of people, institutions, or units that is defined by participation in a program or intervention or by shared personal, social, or health characteristics. Three examples of groups that might be of interest to a surveyor are people who receive an experimental medicine, employees who implement the terms of a flexible work-hours policy for the first time, and schools that try out an innovative adult literacy program. The group that takes part in an untested intervention, such as those just mentioned, is called the *experimental* group. The experimental group is contrasted with one or more *control* groups, which do not participate in the experiment or innovation.

A basic survey design compares experimental and control groups that have been created just for the survey. For example, you can compare people trying out a new medicine (the experimental group) with a group of people using a traditional medicine (the control group) and also with a second group not taking any medicine (a second control group). Sometimes one group serves as its own control; for example, you can survey people just before they take a new medicine and again 1 year later. These two designs are **prospective** because the events of interest occur after the study begins. That is, the study begins and then the effects of the new medicine (or other intervention) on people are surveyed over time, or *longitudinally.*

Another type of longitudinal, prospective survey involves identifying and surveying members of a group who share important characteristics (e.g., severe headaches) and then surveying some or all of the members of the group at least once more. This group, called a **cohort**, can also be compared to a control group.

Retrospective survey designs are concerned with events that have already occurred. For example, you could interview teens between 13 and 17 years of age who get headaches at least once a month and teens of the same age who rarely get headaches and compare the results. The teens with the headaches are called the *cases,* and the teens without headaches constitute the control group. This design is retrospective because the headaches were present before the study was initiated. A useful way to distinguish between prospective and retrospective designs is to focus on the direction of inquiry. If the direction is forward, the design is prospective. If the inquiry follows a path backward through time, the design is retrospective.

✓ Who is eligible?

The **eligibility criteria** separate those who can participate in the survey from those who cannot. Those who are eligible are the target of the survey. The survey's findings can be applied only to the target group.

In Example 1.3 under "Describing," the target of the survey's findings consists of men of differing ages, health, and social characteristics who have had surgery for prostate cancer within the past 2 years. Men who have had chemotherapy or observational treatment or who have had surgery more than 2 years ago are not eligible for inclusion in the survey. Because they are not eligible, the survey's findings about quality of life may not be applicable to these men. A survey's findings are applicable, or generalizable, only to the eligible participants—assuming they participate—because eligible nonparticipants may differ from participants. Nonparticipants' views are likely not as strong, for example; the survey results may be based only or primarily on the views of advocates.

In Example 1.3 under "Comparing—Design 1," the target is schoolchildren in grades 1 through 6. These children are the only ones who are eligible for the survey. Those in kindergarten or grade 7 are not in the target group, and the findings may not apply to them.

The criteria for inclusion in a survey come from three sources: the survey's target population and geographic and temporal proximity. Consider the inclusion criteria in Example 1.4.

Surveyors often set practical inclusion criteria simply to conserve resources. If the survey's participants live close by, then the costs of travel to and from in-person interviews are less than if interviewers or participants must travel relatively long distances. In the case of telephone interviews, local calls cost less than long-distance

EXAMPLE 1.4
Inclusion Criteria:
Target Population, Geography, and Time

Survey	Target Population	Geographic Proximity	Temporal Proximity
Quality of life after prostate cancer surgery	Men who are 65 years of age and older who have had surgery for prostate cancer	Live within 30 miles of the Survey Center	Surgery within past 2 years
Young children's attitudes toward school	Children in grades 1 through 6	Attend one of five elementary schools in the district	Participated in one of two experimental reading programs

calls. By choosing sites with potentially large numbers of eligible respondents, you can simplify the logistics of a survey: Instead of surveying participants in many sites, you can administer the survey instrument in relatively few.

Surveys sometimes have exclusion criteria as well as inclusion criteria, to make sure that no respondents are included who are likely to impair the actual functioning of the survey or skew the data. Consider the kinds of exclusion criteria presented in Example 1.5.

EXAMPLE 1.5
Possible Exclusion Criteria

- Not likely to complete the survey (for reasons such as memory deficits, major psychiatric illness, or severe vision or hearing impairment)

- Unable to read, understand, or write the language of the survey

- Experiences the event of interest only rarely (e.g., has infrequent occurrences of the social, educational, or medical event being studied)

- Presence of only some of the inclusion criteria (e.g., right age and geographic location, but unable to read English)

2 Classification of Designs for Survey Studies

Surveys are systems for collecting information to describe, compare, and predict attitudes, opinions, values, knowledge, and behavior. An essential component of any survey is the design or environmental arrangement in which data are collected, analyzed, and interpreted. Designs for survey studies can be categorized as **experimental** or **descriptive** (sometimes also called **observational**), as described below.

- *Experimental designs:* Experimental survey study designs are those in which the surveyors arrange to compare two or more groups, at least one of which is experimental and the others of which are control (or comparison) groups. The experimental group is given a new or untested innovative program, intervention, or treatment, and the controls are given alternatives. A *group* is any collective unit. Sometimes these units are made up of individuals with common experiences, such as men who have had surgery, children who are in a reading program, or victims of violence; other units are naturally occurring, such as classrooms, businesses, or hospitals.

Concurrent controls in which participants are randomly assigned to groups. Concurrent controls are control groups that are assembled at the same time as the experimental groups against which they are to be compared, such as when 10 of 20 schools are randomly assigned to an experimental group at the same time the other 10 are assigned to a control group. Such an arrangement results in a *randomized controlled trial* or *true experiment.*

Concurrent controls in which participants are not randomly assigned to groups. When the participants in concurrent control groups are not assigned randomly, they are called *nonequivalent controls,* and the resulting studies are *nonrandomized controlled trials* or *quasi-experiments.*

Self-controls. Sometimes measures are taken repeatedly with one group, which thus serves as its own control group. Such self-control studies, which require premeasures and postmeasures, are called *longitudinal* or *before-after* designs.

Historical controls. Studies using historical control groups compare data collected from participants in previous surveys to data collected from current participants.

Combination designs. Some experimental studies employ combinations of different kinds of control groups and survey techniques, such as concurrent controls with or without pre- and postmeasures.

- ■ *Descriptive (observational) designs:* Descriptive study designs, which are also sometimes called *observational designs,* produce information on groups and phenomena that already exist; no new groups are created.

Cross-sectional designs. Cross-sectional surveys gather descriptive data at one fixed point in time. A survey of American voters' current choices is a cross-sectional survey.

Cohorts designs. These forward-looking designs are aimed at gathering data about changes in specific populations, or cohorts. A survey of the aspirations of athletes who participated in the 1996 Olympic Games that is taken in 1996, 2000, and 2004 is a cohort design; in this case the cohort is 1996 Olympians.

Case-control designs. Case-control studies are retrospective; that is, the surveyors go back in time to help explain current phenomena. At least two groups are included in every case-control design. An example is a study in which the medical records of a sample of smokers and a sample of nonsmokers of the same age, health, and socioeconomic status are surveyed and the findings are compared.

Experiments

In experimental studies, surveys can be conducted any number of times before, during, and after a program or intervention. Surveys conducted beforehand serve many important purposes—for example, the survey team may use the data gathered in such surveys to select groups to participate in a program, to check the support for a program, to ensure the comparability of groups, or to serve as a basis from which to monitor change. Some of the uses of surveys as premeasures are illustrated in Example 2.1.

Surveys can also be used during the period when an intervention is being introduced, to measure change, and after the intervention is completed, to measure outcomes and impacts. Some of these uses are illustrated in Example 2.2.

EXAMPLE 2.1
Surveys as Premeasures

To Select Participants

A self-administered questionnaire is given to all parents of children attending a particular school. They are asked to specify the number of years of formal education they have completed in this or any other country. They are also asked to rate their willingness to participate in one of two experimental programs to improve literacy. All of the parents who state that they have completed fewer than 10 years of schooling and who indicate that they are "definitely" willing to participate are considered eligible to participate in a study concerning the two experimental programs.

To Check the Support for a Program

A questionnaire is mailed to all residents of a given town to find out if they are willing to participate in a program aimed at teaching home-based injury prevention. The questionnaire asks the residents if they are willing to be in a control group, if randomly selected.

To Ensure Comparability of Groups

Students in a particular school are assigned to experimental and control groups for a study of a new reading program. Before the start of the experiment, the research team surveys the student participants to gather data that will enable comparison of the ages and reading levels of the members of the two groups, to check that the distribution of participants is similar with respect to these two important variables.

Example 2.1 continued

To Provide a Basis for Monitoring Change

Prisoners who have been selected to participate in a study of the results of a new art therapy program are assigned to either the experimental group or the control group. Before the experiment begins, the researchers interview all participants, using a standardized instrument designed to measure rage. A similar survey will be given after the experimental group completes 6 months of the art therapy program.

EXAMPLE 2.2
Surveys as Interim and Postmeasures

To Measure Change

People over 65 years of age who have been to a particular hospital's emergency room because of a fall are interviewed within 2 weeks of their ER visits and then again 3, 6, and 12 months later. Those in the experimental group received geriatric assessments at the time of their hospital visits; those in the control group did not. The survey team uses the follow-up interviews to compare the two groups with respect to their social, psychological, and physical functioning.

To Measure Outcomes

Prisoners in an art therapy program are interviewed by two psychiatrists within 3 months of completing their course of study. The results are compared with those obtained from interviews with the control group.

Example 2.2 continued

To Measure Impact

Two groups of elderly people, those who received special geriatric assessments after they had gone to a hospital because of fall and those who did not, are surveyed 1, 3, and 5 years later. The purpose of the surveys at 3 and 5 years is to assess and compare the impacts of such assessments over time.

CONCURRENT CONTROLS AND RANDOM ASSIGNMENT

To create groups in a survey study using concurrent controls and random assignment, one must first set up eligibility criteria and then randomly assign eligible "units" to one or more experimental and control groups. The groups can be observed and measured periodically. If the experimental group is observed to differ from the control group in a positive way on important outcome variables (e.g., satisfaction, quality of life, health, knowledge), the experiment is considered successful within certain predefined limits. The units that are randomly assigned may be individuals (e.g., Persons A, B, C, and so on, or Teachers A, B, C, and so on) or clusters of individuals (e.g., schools, residential blocks, hospitals).

In **random assignment** (sometimes called *randomization* or *random allocation*), individuals or clusters of individuals are assigned by chance to the experimental group or a control group. With random assignment, the occurrence of previous events has no value for predicting future events. The alternative to randomization is regulation of the allocation process so that group assignment can be predicted; an example would be assigning people admitted to a hospital on odd days of the month to the experimental group and assigning those admitted on even days to the control group.

Example 2.3 shows one method of randomly assigning units to an experimental group and a control group. The survey team in this example uses a table of random numbers. Such tables are available in most standard statistics texts, or you can generate random numbers easily using most statistical computer programs.

Designs that use concurrent controls and random assignment are also called *randomized trials, randomized controlled trials,* and *true experiments.* Example 2.4 gives two illustrations of their use with random assignment of individuals and of groups or clusters of individuals.

Random selection is different from random assignment. In the second illustration in Example 2.4, the hospitals were randomly selected from all that were eligible. In some surveys, the entire eligible population is used; in others, only a sample of that eligible population is chosen. In most instances, probability sampling methods (such as random sampling) are preferred. Probability sampling methods are those in which all eligible units have a known chance of selection.

EXAMPLE 2.3
Using a Table of Random Numbers to Assign Participants to Groups

Twenty schools are eligible to participate in a trial of a program to improve public speaking skills: 10 are to be in the experimental group and 10 in the control group. If the experimental program is found to be effective in improving participants' skills and confidence, it will be offered to the control schools free of charge.

The survey team places the names of all 20 schools on a list and assigns each a number from 1 to 20 (e.g., John Adams School = 1; Robert Burns School = 2; Joseph Zermatt School = 20). Then, consulting a table of random numbers, they use the first 10 numbers that appear to assign schools to the experimental group. Here is how they make their selections.

Example 2.3 continued

1. *Randomly identify the row.* The researchers place 10 slips of paper numbered 1 through 10 in a jar. They then select one slip from the jar without looking, make a note of the number on the slip, and place the slip back in the jar. They then make a second selection, again noting the number and returning the slip to the jar. The first number drawn is 3 and the second is 5, so they apply these numbers to the following table by going to the block of numbers in the third row down on the far left of the table and then to the fifth row of that block, or number 1 4 5 7 5.

2. *Randomly identify the column.* The researchers again select two numbered slips from the jar, as in the first step. This time they get a 2 and a 1, so they go to the second column of the table and the first row in that column, the number 1 9 7 0 4.

3. *Choose the experimental group.* The researchers find the place in the table where the row (beginning with 1 4 5 7 5) and column (beginning with 1 9 7 0 4) they have found thus far intersect, at 3 5 4 9 0.

4. *Select the schools for the sample.* Because 10 schools are needed for the sample, the researchers must select 10 numbers between 01 and 20 from the table. Moving down column 2, and starting with the numbers below 3 5 4 9 0, the first double-digit number they come to is 70. The numbers they find that

Example 2.3 continued

meet their needs from that point on are 12,
20, 09, 02, 01, 13, 18, 03, 04, and 16. These
are the schools that constitute the experimental group.

1 8 2 8 3	1 9 7 0 4[b]	4 5 3 8 7	2 3 4 7 6	1 2 3 2 3	3 4 8 6 5
4 6 4 5 3	2 1 5 4 7	3 9 2 4 6	9 3 1 9 8	9 8 0 0 5	6 5 9 8 8
1 9 0 7 6	2 3 4 5 3	3 2 7 6 0	2 7 1 6 6	7 5 0 3 2	9 9 9 4 5
3 6 7 4 3	8 9 5 6 3	**1 2 3 7 8**	9 8 2 2 3	2 3 4 6 5	2 5 4 0 8
2 2 1 2 5	1 9 7 8 6	2 3 4 9 8	7 6 5 7 5	7 6 4 3 5	6 3 4 4 2
7 6 0 0 9	7 7 0 9 9	4 3 7 8 8	3 6 6 5 9	7 4 3 9 9	**0 3 4 3 2**
0 9 8 7 8	7 6 5 4 9	8 8 8 7 7	2 6 5 8 7	4 4 6 3 3	7 7 6 5 9
3 4 5 3 4	4 4 4 7 5	5 6 6 3 2	3 4 3 5 0	**0 1 7 6 8**	2 9 0 2 7
8 3 1 0 9	7 5 8 9 9	3 4 8 7 7	2 1 3 5 7	2 4 3 0 0	0 0 8 6 9
8 9 0 6 3	4 3 5 5 5	3 2 7 0 0	7 6 4 9 7	3 6 0 9 9	9 7 9 5 6
				9 4 6 5 6	3 4 6 8 9
0 9 8 8 7	6 7 7 7 0	6 9 9 7 5	5 4 4 6 5	**1 3 8 9 6**	**0 4 6 4 5**
2 3 2 8 0	3 4 5 7 2	9 9 4 4 3	9 8 7 6 5	3 4 9 7 8	4 2 8 8 0
9 3 8 5 6	2 3 0 9 0	2 2 2 5 7	6 7 4 0 0	2 3 5 8 0	2 4 3 7 6
2 1 2 5 6	5 0 8 6 3	5 6 9 3 4	7 0 9 9 3	3 4 7 6 5	3 0 9 9 6
1 4 5 7 5[a]	3 5 4 9 0[c]	2 3 6 4 5	2 2 1 7 9	3 5 7 8 8	3 7 6 0 0
2 3 2 7 6	7 0[d] 8 7 0	**2 0 0 8 7**	6 6 6 6 5	7 8 8 7 6	5 8 0 0 7
8 7 5 3 0	4 5 7 3 8	**0 9 9 9 8**	4 5 3 9 7	4 7 5 0 0	3 4 8 7 5
0 0 7 9 1	3 2 1 6 4	9 7 6 6 5	2 7 5 8 9	9 0 0 8 7	**1 6 0 0 4**
9 9 0 0 3	3 2 5 6 7	**0 2 8 7 8**	3 8 6 0 2	**1 8 7 0 0**	2 3 4 5 5
1 4 3 6 7	6 4 9 9 9	7 8 4 5 3	4 0 0 7 8	5 3 7 2 7	2 8 7 5 9

Explanations:
Numbers in bold = Sample of 10, consisting of numbers between 01 and 20.
a = Two random choices of numbers in a jar yield 1 (column) and 5 (block).
b = Two random choices of numbers in a jar yield 2 (column) and 1 (row).
c = Intersection of first two random choices (superscripts a and b).
d = Start here to get the sample.

EXAMPLE 2.4
Experimental Studies
With Concurrent Controls
and Random Assignment to Groups

1. Comparing Medical and Surgical Therapy

Medical and surgical therapy were compared for patients with stable ischemic heart disease (*ischemia* refers to an insufficient supply of blood to the heart). Over 4 years, half of all eligible patients in each of 10 medical centers were assigned at random to either the medical group or the surgical therapy group. This design can be illustrated as follows:

Intervention		
Medical Center	Surgical Therapy	Medical Therapy
1 (100 patients)	50	50
2 (60 patients)	30	30
3 (120 patients)	60	60
4 (90 patients)	45	45
5 (100 patients)	50	50
6 (90 patients)	45	45
7 (70 patients)	35	35
8 (150 patients)	75	75
9 (150 patients)	75	75
10 (100 patients)	50	50

To find out about length of survival, the researchers compared patients across medical centers (e.g., they compared patients in Medical Center 1 with those in 2, 3, and so on; those in Medical Center 2 with those in 3,

Example 2.4 continued

4, and so on). They also made comparisons of patients in surgical versus medical therapy, regardless of medical center.

No differences were found in survival between and across medical centers and types of therapy. The surgical group had a higher quality of life, as manifested by relief of chest pain, scores on a functional status questionnaire, and reduced need for drug therapy.

2. Changes in Physician Compliance With Practice Guidelines

The investigators used a randomized controlled experimental design to measure changes in individual physician compliance with blood transfusion guidelines following an experimental education program.

Pairs of teaching and community hospitals were randomly selected from all hospitals that met entry criteria (including rates of transfusion for selected procedures and diagnoses) within three health service areas. After randomly selecting one teaching hospital and one community hospital from the entire list, the investigators randomly identified a second hospital of each type from one of the other two health service areas to minimize the risk of experimental contamination due to physicians' practicing at multiple sites within a health service area. The investigators then randomly assigned one surgical service in each matched pair to the study group and the other to the control group; within each hospital, they assigned the medical service to the treatment group opposite from surgery. To measure changes in physician practices, the investigators analyzed the study physicians' compliance with guidelines for transfusion for 6 months before and 6 months following the experimental intervention.

Experimental designs using randomly constituted con-current controls enable you to pinpoint and isolate an inter-vention's outcomes. They are the gold standard, or the preferred designs, for doing scientific research. With a large enough sample, these designs can control nearly all errors or biases from extraneous factors, including those that you do not know about and do not measure. In fact, randomization helps ensure that all groups have, on average, the same dis-tribution of extraneous factors if the sample is large enough.

What are the errors or biases that can lead to false conclu-sions? One of the most potentially damaging biases can come from the method of "selection." Selection bias is pres-ent when a surveyor compares people who are initially dif-ferent from one another and have differing prior risks for the outcome of interest. Suppose a survey is conducted after Schools A and B participate in a comparative test of two approaches to reading. The survey results reveal that chil-dren in School A's reading program (the control) score higher (better) on an attitude-toward-reading inventory than do children in School B (the experiment). Although these results suggest a failed experiment, the two groups may have been different to begin with, even if they appeared to be sim-ilar. For instance, the children in the two schools may be alike in socioeconomic background, reading ability, and the competence of their reading teachers, but they may differ in other important ways. School B, for example, may have a better library, a friendlier librarian, more resources to spend on extraprogram reading, and a social system that reinforces reading among students. To avoid possible bias stemming from the selection process, the survey team should have ran-domly assigned students into experimental and control groups regardless of school.

Biases can arise from unrecognized as well as recognized characteristics of the individuals compared. Randomization is the only known way to control for unknown biases and to distribute them fairly.

Survey study designs using concurrent controls and ran-dom assignment are complex. One issue that often arises concerns the appropriate unit of randomization. Sometimes, for practical purposes, clusters (schools, companies) rather than individuals are chosen for random assignment. You cannot assume, however, that the individuals who form groups are comparable in the same way they would have been had they been randomized as individuals.

Other potential sources of bias include failure to monitor the randomization process adequately and to follow uniform procedures across all groups. It is essential that all members of the survey team be properly trained, and that the quality of the randomization process be monitored carefully.

In some randomized studies, neither the participants nor the investigators know which group is the experimental one and which is the control; these are **double-blind experiments.** When participants do not know which group is which but the investigators do, the experiment is called *blinded.* In many survey studies, it is logistically or ethically difficult to "blind" participants, and this may bias the results. One way to try to reduce such possible bias is to "blind" the persons administering the survey, as illustrated in Example 2.5.

EXAMPLE 2.5
"Blinding" in Experimental Designs

Two groups of employees have completed 4-week training courses to improve selected business skills. The employees were randomly assigned either to the regular course or to the experimental course. A major objective of the experimental course is the improvement of negotiation skills; this topic is not covered in the regular course. At the end of the 4 weeks, all employees are interviewed by specially trained examiners who rate the employees' skills in setting up contracts for the company. Each employee is rated by two examiners, neither of whom knows whether the employee has participated in the experimental course or the regular course.

To maximize the applicability, or **generalizability,** of your survey study results, you should probably conduct experiments in many places with a variety of participants over a number of years. The technical and financial resources needed to conduct concurrently randomized controlled experiments are great, but the potential for sound conclusions justifies the costs. However, despite their scientific virtues, experimental designs with concurrent controls do not automatically fit all survey situations. Studies using these designs do not provide data quickly for use in decision making. Also, randomization is sometimes not ethical, as when a group would be denied an experimental intervention that has a reasonable chance of having more benefits than risks. Finally, you cannot assume that randomization alone will guarantee that your survey will produce "truth." At a minimum, valid survey findings depend on clearly stated purposes, justified samples, accurate data collection, and appropriate statistical analysis and interpretation.

Guidelines for Experimental Designs Involving Randomly Assigned Concurrent Controls

When you are using survey designs with concurrent controls and random assignment, take care to do the following:

1. Define the target population.

2. Choose inclusion and exclusion criteria that are theoretically appropriate and practical.

3. Use probability sampling (such as random sampling) if you are going to survey a sample of eligible participants.

4. Use a table of random numbers, computer-generated list, or other means to ensure that the experimental and control groups are randomly constituted.

5. Monitor the effects of potential errors stemming from inadequate implementation of randomization, lack of uniformity in experimental and control groups, and discovery by participants that they are in the experimental (or control) group.

6. Decide in advance of conducting the survey how you will handle the ethical implications of denying a potentially beneficial intervention to the control group.

7. Be certain that you have the resources to implement and monitor the logistics of a randomized trial or true experiment.

8. Do not rest after you have implemented the design: Check to see that the data collection and analysis methods are equally valid.

CONCURRENT CONTROLS BUT NO RANDOM ASSIGNMENT

Study designs using nonrandomized, concurrent controls (quasi-experimental designs) are those in which at least two already existing groups, one of which is designated experimental, are compared (see Example 2.6).

Concurrent control designs without randomization are easier to implement than experimental designs with randomization. Perhaps the ease with which they can be implemented accounts for the fact that they may be the oldest

EXAMPLE 2.6
Concurrent Controls
but No Random Assignment

1. Studies have shown that children whose places of residence change many times tend to miss more schooling and are at greater risk for significant behavioral problems than are children with stable addresses. Teachers, counselors, and nurses in three schools participated in a program aimed at teaching them how to administer a survey to children who have moved frequently. The purpose of the survey was to gather information that could guide school and health professionals in anticipating potential problems and, when necessary, making effective referrals. Two schools were chosen to act as controls. In the control schools, no special intervention was introduced. At the end of 3 years, children whose families met relocation criteria were surveyed in both sets of schools.

2. A nonrandomized trial was used to test a program intended to reduce the use of antipsychotic drugs in nursing homes. The program was based on the use of behavioral techniques to manage behavior problems and encourage gradual antipsychotic drug withdrawal. Two rural community nursing homes with elevated antipsychotic use were in the experimental group, and two comparable homes were selected as concurrent controls. Residents in both groups of homes had comparable demographic characteristics

Example 2.6 continued

> and functional status, and each group had a
> baseline rate of 29 days of antipsychotic use
> per 100 days of nursing home residence.

design, as illustrated in Example 2.7, which is taken from the Bible's Book of Daniel (1:11-15; King James Version). Random assignment is sometimes infeasible, as would have been so in the case of the "children" who ate the king's meat and those who ate pulse.

As another example, suppose you want to survey prisoners who have participated in a 3-year art therapy program. Each year, 10 prisoners in three facilities will participate in the program; three other facilities have agreed to serve as the control. The primary purpose of the program is to improve

EXAMPLE 2.7
Concurrent Controls
Without Random Assignment:
The Book of Daniel

Then Daniel said to Melzar, . . . Prove thy servants, I beseech thee, ten days; and let them give us pulse [seeds from peas and beans] to eat, and water to drink. Then let our countenances be looked upon before thee, and the countenance of the children that eat of the portion of the king's meat: and as thou seest, deal with thy servants.

So he consented to them in this matter, and proved them ten days. And at the end of ten days their countenances appeared fairer and fatter in flesh than all the children which did eat the portion of the king's meat. Thus Melzar took away the portion of their meat, and the wine that they should drink; and gave them pulse.

prisoners' ability to cope with potentially violent situations by teaching them to use art as one outlet for emotions such as rage and fear. By the end of the third year, 90 prisoners will have participated. In such a study, random assignment would probably be logistically complicated and costly, so you might look for an alternative design.

The use of nonrandomly selected controls, although relatively practical, increases the likelihood that external factors will bias a survey's results. A typical bias associated with nonrandom assignment is *selection bias* or *membership bias*—that is, the characteristics that members of groups share simply because they are in those groups. Preexisting groups usually have not been assembled haphazardly; people come together and form groups precisely because they have something in common. Perhaps they share similar values, attitudes, behaviors, social status, or health status. Examples of groups made up of people who may share important characteristics are people who live in the same neighborhood (they are likely to be similar in their incomes), children who have the same teacher (they may share similar abilities), patients who see a particular physician (they may have a particular medical problem), prisoners at a minimum-security facility (they probably have committed relatively low-level crimes and are not considered to be great threats to society), and prisoners at a maximum-security facility (they have committed crimes at a higher level of seriousness than minimum-security prisoners and are considered to be greater societal threats). Only random assignment can guarantee that two groups are equivalent from the point of view of all variables that may influence a survey's outcomes.

Membership bias can seriously challenge a survey's accuracy. When you use concurrent controls without random assignment, you should administer a premeasure to determine the equivalence of the groups at the start or at baseline on potentially important characteristics. The second case in Example 2.6 illustrates this, reporting that the residents in the two homes had comparable demographic characteristics, functional status, and use of antipsychotics.

Survey researchers often report on the comparability of their groups of interest at baseline by displaying the data in tables. Example 2.8 shows a sample of one such table, which compares the characteristics of two concurrent, nonrandomly assigned groups. The groups are participants in a program aimed at teaching young women parenting skills. You can see from the table that the participants in the program differ in their ages. If age is an important factor for success in the program, the differences that preexist in the two groups pose a serious problem in this design. A variable that is more likely to be present in one group of subjects than in another or that is related to the outcome of interest and confuses, or confounds, the results is called a *confounding variable.*

Statistical methods such as analysis of covariance (ANCOVA) and the Mantel-Haenzel chi-square are available to help you "control for" the influence of confounding vari-

EXAMPLE 2.8
Comparing Baseline
Characteristics in a Table

Characteristics	Experimental (n = 125)	Control (n = 147)
Infant gender, % male	40.0	42.0
Birth weight, ≤1,500 g, %	24.8	23.8
Maternal age, year, %[a]		
15-17	29.6	9.5
18-19	32.8	18.4
20-24	37.6	72.1
Frequent moving, %	24.8	23.8

a. $p < .001$ for those in the experiment compared with those in the control. (For more about the uses of p in tests of significance, see **How to Manage, Analyze, and Interpret Survey Data**, Volume 9 in this series.)

ables when you do not use random assignment. As a rule, however, it is better to control for confounders before you collect survey data—that is, as part of design and sampling—than afterward, during analysis.

SELF-CONTROLS

A design with **self-controls** uses a group of participants to serve as its own comparison. Suppose, for example, that you survey students three times: at the beginning of the year, to find out their attitudes toward community service; immediately after their participation in a 1-year course in which community service is emphasized, to find out the extent to which their attitudes have changed; and at the end of 2 years, to ascertain if any changes found at the time of the second interview have been sustained. In this three-measurement strategy, the interviewed students serve as their own control group. The survey measures the same students once before and twice after the intervention (a new course). Designs of this type are also called *before-and-after* or *pretest-posttest* designs.

Surveys that use self-controls are prone to several biases: Participants may become excited about taking part in an experiment, and this may influence the results; they may mature physically, emotionally, and intellectually; or historical events may intervene. For example, suppose a survey reveals that the students in a 2-year test of a school-based intervention have acquired important attitudes and behaviors and have retained them over time. This desirable result may be due to the intervention, or it may be due to the characteristics of the students, who may have been motivated from the start to learn and have become even more motivated by the realization that they are part of an experimental program. Another possibility is that over the 2-year intervention period the students may have matured intellectually, and this development, rather than the program, is responsible for the learning. Also, historical or external events may have occurred to cloud the effects of the intervention. For example, suppose that during the first year of the intervention the students were exposed to several stimulating lectures given by an inspiring teacher. The students' outstanding performance on subsequent tests may be due as much or more to the lectures as to the new program.

The soundness of self-controlled designs is dependent on the appropriateness of the number and timing of the measurements. To check retention of learning, should you test students once? Twice? At what intervals? A program might appear to be ineffective just because data are gathered too soon, before the hoped-for outcomes have an opportunity to occur.

On their own, self-controls are a relatively weak study design. The addition of a control group can strengthen the usefulness of self-controls, as illustrated in Example 2.9.

EXAMPLE 2.9
Using Combined Self-Control and Concurrent Control Designs to Evaluate the Impacts of Education and Legislation on Children's Use of Bicycle Helmets

An anonymous questionnaire regarding use of bicycle helmets was sent twice to nearly 3,000 children in three counties. The first mailing took place 3 months before the beginning of an educational campaign in County 1 and 3 months before the passage of legislation requiring helmets and the start of an education campaign in County 2. The second mailing took place 9 months after completion of the education campaign in County 1 and 9 months after the combined education-legislation changes in County 2. Two surveys (9 months apart) were also conducted in County 3, the control. County 3 had neither education nor legislation pertaining to the use of bicycle helmets. The following table summarizes the results.

Example 2.9 continued

Percentages of Children Reporting
Who Use Helmets "Always" or "Usually"

	Before Intervention	After Intervention
County 1: Education only	8	13*
County 2: Education and legislation	11	37**
County 3: No intervention	7	8

NOTE: The percentages are small and do not add up to 100% because they represent only the proportion of children answering "always" or "usually." Other responses, such as "rarely," constituted the other choices.
*$p < .01$.
$p < .0001$. (For more about p values, see **How to Manage, Analyze, and Interpret Survey Data, Volume 9 in this series.)

Findings

The proportion of children who reported that they "always" or "usually" wore a helmet increased significantly ($p < .0001$), from 11% before to 37% after in County 2 (education and legislation) and 8% before to 13% after ($p < .01$) in County 1 (education only). The increase of 1% in County 3 was not significant.

Education alone and education combined with legislation were relatively effective; either one or both increased the proportion of children reporting helmet use. The education campaigns may have taught children to give socially acceptable responses on the survey, but single education programs alone have not usually been shown to encourage children to give desirable responses to survey questions. The fact that the control group did not improve suggests that the education and legislation efforts in Counties 1 and 2 were responsible for the improvements. The addition of the control group adds credibility to the survey results.

HISTORICAL CONTROLS

Surveys that use **historical controls** rely on recorded data available from other sources. These data substitute for the data that would come from concurrent controls in other studies.

Historical controls include established norms, such as scores on standardized tests (e.g., the SATs and the MCATs); the results of other surveys conducted with similar groups of people; and vital statistics, such as birthrates and death rates. Historical controls are convenient, and the main source of bias associated with the use of such controls is the potential lack of comparability between the group on which the data were originally collected and the group of concern in the current survey.

Suppose you are concerned with examining the proportion of children from birth through age 7 in your county who have regular sources of medical care. You might ask: How do the children in my county, many of whom are poor, compare with other children in the United States with respect to having regular sources of medical care? To answer this question, you would take the following four steps.

First, survey the children in your county regarding their medical care. *Second,* find out whether comparison data pertaining to other U.S. children are available and whether it is feasible for you to obtain those data. A good way to find out what data are available is to start with city, state, or national health agencies that are responsible for collecting social and health statistics. Another option is to check public and university libraries to find out the types of statistical information they have available to the public and how you can get access to that information.

Third, if information is available and it is feasible for you to obtain it, do so, and then create a worksheet on which you can record the information you have gathered in your survey alongside the information you gain from your other source. Suppose you find useful data from the 1988 U.S. National Interview Survey of Child Health. Then you can prepare a chart like the following:

	Under Age 1 (%)	1-4 Years (%)	5-7 Years (%)
All children			
Family income Under $10,000			
$10,000-$24,999			
$25,000-$39,999			
$40,000 or more			

Fourth, enter your own survey data and the data from your other source into the chart you have created and apply the appropriate statistical techniques (for recommendations about statistical methods you can use when comparing percentages, see **How to Manage, Analyze, and Interpret Survey Data**, Volume 9 in this series). Consider the following hypothetical example:

Percentages of Children in Hypothetical County (HC) and the United States (US) With Regular Sources of Medical Care

	Under Age 1 (%)		1-4 Years (%)		5-7 Years (%)	
	HC	US	HC	US	HC	US
All children	89.9	87.2	92.3	84.5	89.5	90.8
Family income						
Under $10,000	83.7	82.4	86.7	88.3	87.6	88.8
$10,000-$24,999	95.7	92.7	91.3	92.5	88.5	88.3
$25,000-$39,999	95.3	91.3	96.1	94.6	90.1	89.4
$40,000 or more	95.3	94.4	97.7	96.5	96.7	94.7

SOURCE: Statistics for the U.S. portion obtained from the 1988 U.S. National Interview Survey of Child Health.

WARNING

 When interpreting the data in the table, remember that they were collected in 1988, and many changes in health care may have occurred since then.

COMBINATIONS

All survey studies using experimental designs compare one or more groups that are surveyed before, during, and/or after any intervention. There are several possible variations on these basic elements. A common design in medical studies is the crossover, in which one group is assigned to the experimental group and the other to the control. After a certain length of time, the experimental and control groups are withdrawn for a "washout" period, during which no treatment is given. Each of the groups is then given the alternative treatment: The group that was experimental becomes the control and the group that was the control becomes the experimental.

Solomon Four-Group Design

The **Solomon four-group design** is a randomized control trial in which some groups receive pre- and postmeasures and some receive only postmeasures. This is illustrated in Example 2.10. In this example, Groups 1 and 3 participated in a new program, but Groups 2 and 4 did not. Suppose the new program aimed to improve employees' awareness of health hazards at their place of work. Using the four-group design (and assuming an effective program), the survey should find the following:

1. In Group 1, awareness should be greater on the postmeasure than on the premeasure.

2. More awareness should be observed in Group 1 than in Group 2.

3. Group 3's postmeasure should show more awareness than Group 2's premeasure.

4. Group 3's postmeasure should show more awareness than Group 4's postmeasure.

EXAMPLE 2.10
The Solomon Four-Group Design

Group 1	Premeasure	Program	Postmeasure
Group 2	Premeasure		Postmeasure
Group 3		Program	Postmeasure
Group 4			Postmeasure

This design is a randomized controlled trial, and it incorporates self- and concurrent controls. The use of random and nonrandom assignment in the same study is illustrated in Example 2.11.

EXAMPLE 2.11
Random and Nonrandom Assignment in a Single Study

Four of 14 eligible participating high schools were grouped into two pairs of demographically similar schools (this is nonrandom assignment). A 30% sample of 9th-grade classrooms (16 classrooms totaling 430 students) in the first member of the two pairs of schools was selected at random from the total 9th-grade general education enrollment in these two schools to receive a special AIDS-preventive curriculum in the first semester of the academic year. A 20% random sample of 9th-grade classrooms (10 classrooms totaling 251 students) in the second member of the two pairs served as the comparison or control group and received no formal AIDS curriculum at school that semester. Similarly, a 30% sample of 11th-grade classrooms (13 classrooms totaling 309 students) in the second member of the two pairs of schools was selected at random from the total 11th-grade general education enrollment in these two schools to receive the special prevention curriculum in the second semester of the same academic year, and a 20% random sample of 11th-grade classrooms (13 classrooms totaling 326 students) in the first member of the two pairs served as the comparison or control group. A higher proportion of intervention than comparison students was sampled so that more students would be exposed to the special curriculum. The study design also ensured that none of the four participating high schools would be denied implementation of the special curriculum at grade 9 or 11.

Two Kinds of Factorial Designs

Factorial designs may be descriptive (observational) or experimental.

Descriptive factorial designs. A **descriptive factorial design** lays out all combinations of several independent variables at one time. Suppose your organization is interested in improving managers' leadership skills. You decide to survey employees to find out which of the current managers are most effective and what makes them so effective. You plan to use the findings to guide the development of a leadership-training program.

You have a hunch that employees use different criteria to evaluate male managers and female managers. You also think that they apply different criteria to managers who are 40 years of age and younger and those who are 41 and older. Your experience at the company suggests that, regardless of management style, older male managers are generally perceived to be more effective than younger male managers or any female managers. To find out if this is true, you decide to categorize managers as primarily democratic (those who use a participatory decision-making style) or autocratic (those who make decisions with a minimum of staff consultation). To measure manager style, you use a validated self-administered survey of leadership styles.

You survey employees to find out how and if the gender or age of the manager and management style affect staff perceptions of effectiveness (see Example 2.12). This is a 2 (democratic or autocratic) × 2 (male or female) × 2 (40 and younger or 41 and older) factorial design. With this design, you can study **main effects,** or the effects of each factor (e.g., democratic versus autocratic) on the dependent variable (perceptions of effectiveness), as well as **interaction effects,** or the effects on the dependent variable that occur as a result of the interaction between two or more independent variables (e.g., gender and age).

EXAMPLE 2.12
Descriptive Factorial Design:
Effective Managers

Dependent variable: Employees' perceptions of managers' effectiveness (as measured by a validated survey of effectiveness)

Independent variables (or factors):

1. Style (democratic or autocratic)

2. Gender (male or female)

3. Age (40 and younger or 41 and older)

	Democratic		Autocratic	
	Male	Female	Male	Female
40 and under				
41 and older				

With respect to employees' perceptions of effectiveness, the questions you ask about main effects are as follows:

1. How do democratic managers compare with autocratic managers?

2. How do men compare with women?

3. How do managers 40 and under compare with managers who are 41 and older?

Do differences exist that are due not to style or gender or age alone, but rather to interactions between or among them? The questions you ask about such interaction effects include the following:

1. How do male (or female) democratic managers 40 years of age and younger compare with male (or female) democratic managers 41 years of age or older?

2. How do male (or female) autocratic managers 40 years of age and younger compare with male (or female) autocratic managers 41 years of age or older?

3. How do male democratic (or autocratic) managers 40 years of age and younger (or 41 years of age and older) compare with female democratic (or autocratic) managers 40 years of age and younger (or 41 years of age and older)?

Experimental factorial designs. Factorial designs may be **experimental**. Suppose that you are interested in comparing the effectiveness of cognitive behavioral therapy (CBT) with the effectiveness of behavior modification (BM) for improving relationships between fathers and their teenage sons. Three churches agree to participate in your study and also agree to assign father-son pairs at random to CBT or BM. You survey all participants before and after participation. The design is illustrated in Example 2.13.

The numbers in the cells in the example are the identification numbers of the father-son pairs, which are assigned at random to one of two counseling methods (CBT or BM). If the pairs were not assigned at random, you would still have a factorial design. In this case you have a 2 (churches) × 2 (counseling methods) factorial design.

Experimental designs with three or more factors or independent variables are possible. If you are testing to see if there are differences in outcomes, as in the study illustrated in Example 2.13, you must be certain that you have enough people in each cell so that if differences exist, you will have the power to uncover them. If you need many people, you must plan carefully how you will recruit them and then keep them in the study. Recruiting and maintaining a large number of survey participants can be difficult, time-consuming, and costly.

EXAMPLE 2.13
Experimental Factorial Design: Counseling Fathers and Sons

Church 1		Church 2		Church 3	
CBT	BM	CBT	BM	CBT	BM
1	2	4	1	2	1
6	3	5	2	5	3
7	4	8	3	6	4
8	5	9	6	7	8
9	12	11	7	10	8
11	10	12	10	11	12

NOTE: CBT = cognitive behavioral therapy; BM = behavior modification.

To complicate matters, you may prejudice the results if you make many comparisons. Suppose you have three independent variables or factors (e.g., gender), each with two levels (e.g., male and female). You then have the possibility of 8 comparisons (2 × 2 × 2). If one factor has two levels, another has three, and the third has four, you end up with 24 comparisons (2 × 3 × 4). Just by chance alone, the probability is quite high that you will find that one or more of the comparisons are statistically significant. You can handle some of this during data analysis, but you should be aware of the possibility beforehand.

Descriptions (or Observations)

CROSS-SECTIONAL DESIGNS

Studies using cross-sectional designs result in portraits of one or many groups at one point in time. Cross-sectional designs are used frequently with standard survey-based measurement (that is, mail and self-administered questionnaires and in-person and telephone interviews) and are themselves sometimes called survey designs. Example 2.14 lists six illustrative uses of survey-based measurement and cross-sectional designs.

EXAMPLE 2.14
Surveys and Cross-Sectional Designs

1. A face-to-face interview with refugees to find out their immediate fears and aspirations

2. A questionnaire mailed to consumers to find out their perceptions of the quality of the goods and services they receive when ordering by catalog

3. A telephone interview with people who have undergone surgery to find out what has happened since their last hospitalization

4. A mailed questionnaire with telephone follow-up to find out if residents are prepared properly for emergencies such as fire, flood, and earthquake

5. An interview combined with observations to determine how many children use bicycle helmets over a 2-week period

Example 2.14 continued

6. Interviews conducted over 1 month to find out teenagers' views of the quality of their education in 10 schools

A cross-sectional design provides a portrait of a group during one time period, now or in the past. Sometimes such designs rely on more than one type of survey measure. In the samples of survey types listed in Example 2.14, mail and telephone surveys are used to find out about residents' emergency preparedness, and observations and interviews are combined to collect data on bicycle helmet use among children.

A cross-sectional design that uses random or probability samples is much more likely to have a study population that is representative of the larger target population. For example, suppose you want to conduct a cross-sectional survey about the joys of jogging as perceived by men over 45 years of age. A random sample of 100 men over 45 who jog three or more times each week is more likely to be representative of jogging men over 45 than a selection of the first 100 jogging men who use the Sports Medicine Clinic. Men who come to the clinic may have more injuries, may be more "sports-minded," and may have more time to visit clinics than do men in a random sample. These characteristics (and others that cannot be anticipated) can affect the applicability of the survey's results to the target: men over 45 years old who jog three or more times each week.

Although the result of a cross-sectional design is a group portrait at one point in time, the survey itself may take several weeks or even months to complete. For instance, take two of the studies listed in Example 2.14: Finding out about children's use of bicycle helmets might take 2 weeks, and uncovering teenagers' views might require 1 month. Longer survey periods are necessary with larger samples and when you need to conduct follow-ups. When you are working with very large groups and long periods of data collection, you must define the period to be covered by the survey. For example, consider the case of a yearlong survey of the lifestyles of 10,000 people. Over the course of the 12-month survey period, the very first people surveyed may lose or gain jobs, and this factor may influence their lifestyles. Also, over the span of a year, events outside the scope of the survey, such as economic recession and political upheaval, may affect participants' lifestyles. To help ensure a uniform set of responses, you need to set time limits within your survey, as illustrated in Example 2.15.

EXAMPLE 2.15
Using Time Limits in Surveys

Item from a past U.S. Census questionnaire:

List on the numbered line below the name of each person living here on *Sunday, April 1,* including all persons staying here who have no other home. If EVERYONE at this address is staying here temporarily and usually lives somewhere else, follow the instructions given below.

COHORT DESIGNS

A **cohort** is a group of people who have something in common and who remain part of the group over an extended period of time. In public health research, cohort studies are used to investigate the factors that put individuals at risk for particular diseases as well as the causes of diseases. Such studies include data collection on the incidence and natural histories of the diseases of interest and the prognoses associated with those diseases.

Cohort designs are prospective designs because the direction of inquiry is forward (i.e., they ask, What will happen?). Studies using cohort designs require two groups: the cohort and the control. A cohort design might be used, for example, in a study aimed at examining the consequences of living with asthma over a 10-year period. To implement such a design, the investigator would survey people with and without asthma and compare the results. (Without a control group, this would be termed a *case series.*)

Cohort designs sometimes make use of archival data— that is, data from medical, legal, financial, or other kinds of records. For example, if you were conducting a study of the consequences of living with asthma (and assuming access to complete and accurate records), you might review the medical records of people who developed asthma 10 years ago and follow their recorded progress over time. Notice that, although you are using historical data (the events already happened and are recorded), the direction of inquiry is forward, and thus the study is prospective in design.

Cohort study designs come in two varieties: A Type A cohort design focuses on the same population each time survey data are collected, although the samples may be different, and a Type B cohort design, sometimes called a panel study, focuses on the same sample every time.

- *Type A cohorts: different samples from the same population.* With a Type A cohort design, you can conduct five surveys of the lifestyles of members of a particular high school's class of 1994 over a period of 10 years. Every 2 years, you draw a sample from the entire population of the school's 1994 graduates. In this way, your samples may include some individuals who are asked to complete all five surveys; others will not be chosen to participate at all. Among the most famous cohort studies is the Framingham, Massachusetts, study of cardiovascular disease begun by researchers in 1948 to investigate factors associated with heart disease. More than 6,000 people in Framingham agreed to participate in follow-up interviews and physical examinations every 2 years. Some of the children of members of the original cohort are also now being studied.

- *Type B cohorts: same samples.* Type B cohorts or panels are typically used during election campaigns. Researchers monitor participants' preferences for candidates and views on issues over time and compare the characteristics of particular candidates' supporters and nonsupporters. Investigators also use Type B cohorts to study social, intellectual, and health development in infants and children, as illustrated in Example 2.16.

EXAMPLE 2.16
Cohort Design to Study
Development in Infants and Children

A cohort composed of infants born in five medical centers was selected for a study. Inclusion criteria were as follows: An infant was considered to be in the cohort if he or she weighed no more than 2,500 grams (5.5 pounds) at birth, had a gestational age (the age from conception to birth) of no more than 37 weeks, and was at the postconceptual age of 40 weeks in the period from January to October. Infants with health or congenital conditions were excluded from the study, as were infants whose mothers were under 15 years of age or 25 years or older, could not communicate in English, or were diagnosed with psychiatric illness or alcohol or other drug abuse.

Surveys and assessments were made when each infant was 40 weeks old and at 4, 8, 12, 18, 24, 30, and 36 months gestational age. The table below compares the development scores of the infants in the cohort at 3 years of age.

Example 2.16 continued

Characteristic	Intelligence Scores Mean (SD)[a]	Number of Behavior Problems Mean (SD)	Health Rating Index Mean (SD)
Infant gender			
Male	81.0 (17.7)	30.2 (13.5)**	26.7 (5.2)
Female	81.3 (14.6)	25.8 (11.3)	27.7 (4.4)
Birth weight (grams)			
More than 1,500	79.9 (14.9)	29.5 (12.7)	26.4 (5.3)
Less than 1,500	81.6 (16.3)	27.1 (12.3)	27.5 (4.6)
Maternal age (years)			
15-17	78.2 (12.0)	29.8 (12.7)	27.0 (4.1)
18-19	81.6 (13.3)	29.6 (12.9)	27.4 (5.1)
20-24	81.9 (18.0)	26.2 (12.0)	27.3 (4.9)
Family in poverty			
Yes	77.3 (14.2)*	29.5 (13.4)**	27.1 (5.1)
No	87.6 (16.8)	25.0 (10.4)	27.1 (5.1)
Frequent moving			
Yes	80.2 (13.8)	32.0 (13.9)**	27.4 (4.1)
No	81.5 (16.7)	26.3 (11.6)	27.2 (5.0)

a. *SD* = standard deviation, which is a measure of dispersion or spread around the mean or average.
* $p < .01$—intelligence scores: yes poverty versus no.
**$p < .001$—behavior problems: males versus females; yes poverty versus no; yes moving versus no.

In this cohort of infants, males had significantly more behavior problems than did females. Infants in poverty had significantly lower intelligence scores and more behavior problems. Children who moved frequently had significantly more behavior problems.

Cohort studies sometimes use more than one group. For example, suppose you want to find out if jogging leads to osteoarthritis, a painful condition that affects weight-bearing joints such as the knees and lumbar spine. You might take a group of men over 50 years of age, divide them into a "runners" group and a "nonrunners" group, and collect baseline data. After a period of time—say, 5 years—you can measure if any differences exist in the development or progression of the disorder.

Cohort studies can be expensive because they are longitudinal, requiring measurement at several points in time. They are also subject to biases that can stem from the method of selection (e.g., those who are chosen and willing to participate may be inherently different from the remainder of the cohort who are not willing). Type B cohorts (panels) are also prone to loss of data, with incomplete information collected on important variables or no data collected at all after a certain point in time.

CASE-CONTROL DESIGNS

Case-control designs are retrospective. Investigators use them to help explain why a phenomenon currently exists by comparing two groups, one of which is involved in the phenomenon. For example, you might use a case-control design to help understand the social, demographic, and attitudinal variables that distinguish people who suffer frequent headaches from those who do not.

The cases in case-control designs are individuals who have been chosen on the basis of some characteristic or outcome (such as frequent headaches). The controls are individuals without the characteristic or outcome. The investigator analyzes and compares the histories of both groups in an attempt to uncover one or more characteristics that are present in the cases but not in the controls.

In selecting participants for a case-control study, it is important to avoid creating case and control groups that are decidedly different from each other—with, say, members of one group being older or smarter than members of the other. Investigators often use matching in case-control designs to guard against the possible appearance of confounding variables. For example, in a case-control study of people with frequent headaches, the participants in the two groups should be selected so that they are similar in age, education, and the duration and severity of their headaches (whether or not those headaches are frequent, as in the case group, or infrequent, as in the control). Example 2.17 illustrates the use of case-control designs in surveys.

EXAMPLE 2.17
A Case-Control Design

The National Teacher Corps was created in 1962 to train highly qualified individuals to enter the teaching profession. On the occasion of the Corps' 30th anniversary, a study was conducted to find out why some people the Corps had trained continued to teach and others had changed careers. People who had chosen teaching as their career (the cases) were matched to the controls on age, gender, educational background, and other social and demographic variables. The controls consisted of people who taught for 2 or fewer years after completing the Teacher Corps training program.

Eligible participants were mailed a 100-item questionnaire that asked for information on their perceptions of their satisfaction in their current jobs, willingness to take risks, religious preferences, and living arrangements. The academic records of the two groups before and after their participation in the Corps training were also compared.

Epidemiologists and other health workers often use case-control designs to gain insight into the causes and consequences of disease. These designs are generally less time-consuming and expensive to implement than are cohort designs. Matching is intuitively appealing and feasible.

Case-control designs have their problems, however. First, the groups of cases and controls are selected from two separate populations. Because of this, you cannot be certain that the groups are comparable with respect to extraneous factors such as motivation, cultural beliefs, and other expectations (some of which you may not know). Also, the data for case-control designs are historical, and they often come from incomplete or otherwise inadequate records. Researchers sometimes obtain data by asking people to recall past events and habits. Memory is often unreliable, however, and this introduces mistakes into the data.

Internal and External Validity

A design with **external validity** produces results that apply to the survey's target population. For example, an externally valid survey of the preferences of airline passengers over 45 years of age will result in findings that apply to all airline passengers of that age.

A design is **internally valid** if it is free of nonrandom error or bias. A study design must be internally valid to be externally valid and to produce accurate findings. To ensure your study design's internal validity, you must avoid the common risks noted in the following checklist.

Internal Invalidity:
Checklist of Risks to Avoid

✓ Maturation

Maturation refers to changes within individuals that result from natural, biological, or psychological development. For example, in a 5-year study of a

---

preventive health education program for high school students, the students may mature intellectually and emotionally, and this new maturity may be more important than the program in producing changes in health behavior.

✓ Selection

Selection refers to how people were chosen for the survey and, if they participate in an experiment, how they were assigned to groups. For a survey to avoid selection bias, every eligible person or unit must have an equal, nonzero chance of being included.

✓ History

Historical events may occur that can bias a study's results. For example, suppose a national campaign has been created to encourage people to make use of preventive health care services. If a change in health insurance laws favoring reimbursement for preventive health care should occur at the same time as the campaign, it may be difficult to separate the effects of the campaign from the effects of increased access to care created by more favorable reimbursement for health care providers.

✓ Instruments

Unless the measures (or instruments) that are used to collect data are dependable, you cannot be sure that the findings are accurate. For example, in a before-after design, an easier postmeasure than premeasure will lead to the conclusion, which may be erroneous, that the intervention has been effective. Also, untrained but lenient observers or test administrators might rule in favor of an intervention's effectiveness, whereas untrained but harsh observers or test administrators might rule against it.

✓ Statistical regression

Suppose participants are chosen to receive an intervention designed to foster tolerance. The basis for their selection was their extreme views, as measured by a survey. A second administration of the survey (without any intervention) may appear to suggest that the participants' views have somehow softened, but, in fact, this result may be a statistical artifact called (statistical) **regression toward the mean.** Regression effects are caused by factors such as imperfect test-retest correlation.

✓ Attrition

Attrition refers to the loss of study participants and the data they could have provided. People may not complete surveys because they move away, become ill, or become bored with participating, among other reasons. Sometimes, participants who continue to provide complete survey data throughout a long study are different from those who do not.

Risks to external validity are most often consequences of the ways in which participants or respondents are selected and assigned to groups. For example, respondents in an experimental situation may answer questions atypically because they know they are in a special experiment; this is called the *Hawthorne effect.* External validity is also at risk just because respondents are tested, surveyed, or observed. They may become alert to the kinds of behaviors that are expected or favored. Some sources of external invalidity to avoid are shown in the following checklist.

External Invalidity:
Checklist of Risks to Avoid

✓ Reactive effects of testing

A premeasure can sensitize participants to the aims of an intervention. Suppose two groups of junior high school students are eligible to participate in a program intended to teach ethics. Members of the first group are surveyed regarding their perspectives on selected ethics issues and then are shown a film about young people from different backgrounds faced with ethical dilemmas. Students in the second group are just shown the film. It would not be surprising if students in the first group performed better on a postmeasure if only because the group's members were sensitized to the purpose of the film by the questions on the premeasure.

✓ Interactive effects of selection

Interactive effects of selection occur when an intervention and the participants are a unique mixture, one that may not be found elsewhere. Suppose a school volunteers to participate in an experimental program to improve the quality of students' leisure-time activities. The characteristics of the school (some of which may be related to the fact that school officials volunteered for the experiment) may interact with the program so that the two together form a unique situation; the particular blend of school and intervention can limit the applicability of the findings.

✓ Reactive effects of innovation

Sometimes the environment of an experiment is so artificial that all who participate are aware that something special is going on and behave uncharacteristically.

✓ Multiple-program interference

It is sometimes difficult to isolate the effects of an experimental intervention because of participants are also involved in other complementary activities or programs.

Example 2.18 illustrates how internal and external validity are affected in two different designs. The table that follows the example displays the benefits, limitations, and potential for bias found in nine commonly used study designs.

EXAMPLE 2.18
How the Choice of Design May Affect Internal and External Validity

Concurrent Controls Without Random Assignment

Description: The Food Allergy Mediation Alliance (FAMA) offers a yearlong program for people with food allergies. Eligible people can enroll in one of two variations of the program. To find out if participants are satisfied with the quality of the two variations, the survey team has both groups complete an in-depth questionnaire at the end of the year and compares the results.

Comment: The internal validity of this design is poten-

Example 2.18 continued

tially marred by the fact that the participants in the groups may be different from one another at the beginning of the program. More severely allergic persons may choose one program over the other, for example. Also, because of such initial differences, the attrition rate may be affected. The survey team's failure to create randomly constituted groups and thus avoid the interactive effects of selection jeopardizes the study's external validity.

Concurrent Controls With Randomization

Description: The Make-A-Wish Trust commissioned an evaluation of three different interventions for visually impaired children. The survey team randomly assigned eligible children to one of the three interventions, collected baseline data, and conducted a 3-year investigation of the effectiveness and efficiency of the interventions. At the end of the 3 years, the team had the children examined to determine their functioning on a number of variables, including school performance and behavior at home and at school. The survey team also interviewed the children extensively throughout the study. They compared the results of the children's examinations and interviews with those obtained from a study of visually impaired children who had participated in a similar experiment in another part of the country.

Comment: This design is internally valid. Because the researchers assigned the children randomly to each intervention, any sources of change that might compete with the intervention's impact would affect all three groups equally. To improve external validity, the survey team will compare the findings from a study of other children with those from the Make-A-Wish Trust study. This additional comparison does not guarantee that the

Example 2.18 continued

results will hold for a third group of children. Another consideration is that school administrators and staff may not spend as much money as usual, because they know the study involves measuring efficiency (reactive effects of innovation). Finally, we do not know whether or how baseline data collection affected the children's performance and interviews (interaction between testing and intervention).

Nine Commonly Used Study Designs

Design	Benefits	Limitations	Potential for Bias or Invalidity
Concurrent controls and random assignment (randomized controlled or control trial; true experiment)	If properly conducted, can establish the extent to which a program caused its outcomes	Proper implementation requires resources and methodological expertise	*Internal validity:* Excellent *External validity:* If a premeasure is given, possibility of reactive effects of testing; reactive effects of innovation
Concurrent controls without randomizatio n (quasi-experimental)	Easier to implement than a randomized control trial	A wide range of potential biases may occur because without an equal chance of selection, participants in the program may be systematically different from those in the control group	*Internal validity:* Selection, attrition, cannot be sure about maturation *External validity:* Interactive effects of selection
Self-controls (pretest-posttest)	Relatively easy to implement logistically Provides data on change	Must be certain that measurements are appropriately timed Without a control group, you cannot tell if effects are also present in other groups	*Internal validity:* Maturation, history, instrumentation, and interaction of selection with other factors; regression a possibility *External validity:* Interaction of selection, reactive effects of testing, and possibly reactive effects of innovation

Design	Benefits	Limitations	Potential for Bias or Invalidity
Historical controls	Easy to implement; unobtrusive	Must make sure that "normative" comparison data are applicable to participants	*Internal validity:* Selection, attrition, interaction of selection with other factors; cannot be sure about maturation *External validity:* Interactive effects of selection
Solomon four-group	Rigorous design that permits inferences about causes Guards against the effects of the premeasure on subsequent performance	Need to have enough participants to constitute four groups Expensive to implement	*Internal validity:* Excellent *External validity:* Possibility of interaction of selection and reactive effects of innovation
Factorial	Can be used to study a range of main effects and interactions	May need a very large sample size to study interactions Because of the large number of combinations of questions that may be answered, significant findings may occur by chance	*Internal validity:* If participants are randomly selected or assigned to groups, excellent to very good; otherwise, selection *External validity:* Interactive effects of selection, reactive effects of testing, and possibly reactive effects of innovation

Design	Benefits	Limitations	Potential for Bias or Invalidity
Cross-sectional	Provides baseline information on survey participants and descriptive information about the intervention	Offers a picture of participants and program at one point in time	*Internal validity:* If survey is lengthy, then history and maturation; selection, attrition *External validity:* Only if sample is representative are findings applicable to population
Cohort	Provides longitudinal or follow-up information	Can be expensive because they are relatively long-term studies Participants who are available over time may differ in important ways from those who are not	*Internal validity:* Maturation, history, instrumentation, and interaction of selection with other factors; regression a possibility *External validity:* Interaction of selection and the intervention; reactive effects of testing and possibly reaction to innovation

Design	Benefits	Limitations	Potential for Bias or Invalidity
Case-control	Can provide insights into the causes and consequences of disease Generally less time-consuming and expensive than cohorts	The compared groups of cases and controls are selected from two separate populations, and you cannot be certain that the groups are comparable with respect to extraneous factors (some of which you may not know) Data often come from records, which may be incomplete or otherwise inadequate	*Internal validity:* Selection, attrition, interaction of selection with other factors; cannot be sure about maturation *External validity:* Interactive effects of selection and intervention

Exercises

1. A team of experts spent 5 days interviewing all part-time employees. Which of the following describes their study's design? *Circle one choice.*

Cross-sectional	1
Self-control	2
Concurrent controls without randomization	3
Historical controls	4

2. The goals and aspirations of the 1990 graduates of the three major types of high schools (arts and sciences, vocational, and technical) are followed over 10 years. Each year, the 1990 graduates are interviewed and videotaped. Which of the following study designs is being used? *Circle one choice.*

Case-control	1
Cohort	2
Self-control	3
Quasi-experiment	4

3. What are the threats to internal and external validity of these two survey designs?

   a. The ABC Sales Company experimented with a program to help minorities and women get and keep higher-paying jobs. Human resources staff interviewed all employees and examined records to collect data on the program's effectiveness.

   b. An evaluation of three 1-month rehabilitation programs for patients with heart disease was conducted. Patients were free to choose which of the three programs they would participate in. The evaluation team collected information on whether patients' knowledge of their condition and self-confidence had improved. To answer the question, patients in each program were surveyed before and after program participation.

ANSWERS

1. Cross-sectional

2. Cohort

3. a. Internal validity may be affected by historical events, such as new legislation, that may occur at the same time as the program; these events may be more influential than the program. Also, employees may change job ranks

naturally over time. Finally, the people who remain employed and in the program may be inherently different (e.g., more skilled) from others who are fired or move away. External validity may be influenced by the reactive effects of innovation.

b. Selection is a possible risk to internal validity because participants in the three groups may have been different from one another at the beginning of the programs. For example, healthier people may have tended to choose one program over the other two. Also, there may have been different attrition rates in the three groups. The external validity is limited by a number of factors, including the reactive effects of innovation, interactive effects of selection, and possible multiple-program interference.

Suggested Readings

Bernard, H. R. (2000). *Social research methods: Qualitative and quantitative approaches.* Thousand Oaks, CA: Sage.

Great overview of social research methods; offers a little bit of everything. Chapter 4 provides an overview of designs with good examples.

Campbell, D. T., & Stanley, J. C. (1963). *Experimental and quasi-experimental designs for research.* Chicago: Rand McNally.

Classic book on differing research designs. Describes threats to internal and external validity in detail and presents important discussion of issues pertaining to generalizability and how to get at "truth."

Dawson, B., & Trapp, R. G. (2000). *Basic and clinical biostatistics* (3rd ed.). New York: McGraw-Hill.

Basic and essential primer on the use of statistics in medicine and medical care settings. Discusses study designs in medical research and their advantages and disadvantages and gives examples of the uses of different designs.

Fink, A. (1993). *Evaluation fundamentals: Guiding health programs, research, and policy.* Newbury Park, CA: Sage.

Discusses survey design, sampling, analysis, and reporting from the point of view of program evaluators, whose work requires many of the same skills needed by survey researchers. Chapter 3 covers the range of designs that are useful in program evaluation. Discusses the evaluation design report as well as the roles of independent variables in design and sampling.

Trochim, W. M. K. (2000). *The research methods knowledge base* (2nd ed.). Cincinnati, OH: Atomic Dog.

Comprehensive textbook (available online at trochim.human.cornell.edu/kb) that addresses all of the topics in a typical introductory undergraduate or graduate course in social research methods. Covers the entire research process, including formulating research questions and research design.

Glossary

Attrition—The reduction of numbers of participants in a survey owing to their failure to complete all or parts of the survey instrument; results in loss of data.

Case controls—Control groups formed from retrospective surveys of previous study findings. For example, a study comparing survey findings from a new sample of smokers and nonsmokers to a survey of the past medical records of a sample of smokers and nonsmokers of the same age, health, and socioeconomic status uses a case-control design.

Cohort design—A study design concerned with a particular cohort, or group. Cohort designs can be retrospective, or look back over time (a historical cohort), if the events being studied actually occurred before the onset of the surveys; they can also be forward-looking, or prospective, seeking data about changes in specific populations.

Concurrent controls—Control groups assembled at the same time as the experimental groups with which they are compared. For example, when 10 of 20 schools are randomly assigned to an experimental group and the other 10 are assigned to a control at the same time, the result is a randomized controlled trial or true experiment. When participants in concurrent control groups are not randomly assigned, the results are called nonrandomized controlled trials, quasi-experiments, or nonequivalent controls.

Cross-sectional survey—A survey that provides descriptive data at one fixed point in time (e.g., a survey of American voters' current choices).

Descriptive designs (or observational designs)—Designs for surveys that produce information on groups and phenomena that already exist; no new groups are created in the survey study.

Descriptive factorial designs—Survey designs that lay out all combinations of several independent variables at one time.

Design—The intentional arrangement of the environment in which a survey takes place (the environment consists of the individuals or groups of people, places, activities, or objects that are to be surveyed).

Double-blind experiment—An experiment in which neither participants nor investigators know which group is the experimental one and which is the control.

Eligibility criteria—Criteria used to establish who can participate in the survey from who cannot.

Experimental designs—Designs characterized by the comparison of two or more groups, at least one of which is experimental and the others of which are control (or comparison) groups.

External validity—A form of validity that is achieved when the survey's results apply to the survey's target population.

Generalizability—The applicability of a survey's findings to populations and places other than those involved in the survey.

Group—An assembly of people, institutions, or units that is defined by shared participation in a program or intervention or by shared personal, social, or health characteristics.

Historical controls—Control groups formed from data collected from participants in other surveys.

Historical events—Events outside of the survey study that may bias the study's results. For example, a national campaign aimed at encouraging people to make use of preventive health care services may bias a study of a particular group's use of such services.

Instruments—The measures used to collect survey data. A poorly designed survey instrument is a threat to internal validity, because unless the measures used to collect data are dependable, one cannot be sure that the findings are accurate.

Interaction effects—The effects on the dependent variable that occur as a result of the interaction between two or more independent variables (e.g., gender and age).

Interactive effects of selection—Effects that can occur when an intervention and the participants create a unique mixture, a combination that may not be found elsewhere. Such effects constitute a threat to external validity.

Internally valid designs—Designs that are free of nonrandom error or bias. A study design must be internally valid to be externally valid and to produce accurate findings.

Main effects—The effects of each factor (e.g., democratic versus autocratic) on the dependent variable (e.g., perceptions of effectiveness).

Maturation—Changes within individuals that result from natural, biological, or psychological development.

Measurable objective—An objective about which two or more people easily agree regarding all the words and terms used to describe its purposes.

Multiple-program interference—Interference with study findings that can occur when the possibility exists that participants are also involved in other complementary activities or programs. Such interference constitutes a threat to external validity.

Observational designs—See **Descriptive designs**

Prospective designs—Study designs in which the events of interest occur after the study begins. For example, a study of the effects of a new medicine begins, and then the effects of the medicine on people are surveyed over time, or longitudinally.

Random assignment (or randomization, or random allocation)—The assignment of individuals or clusters of individuals by chance to the experimental group or the control group. When participants are randomly assigned, the occurrence of previous events has no value in predicting future events.

Reactive effects of innovation—Effects that may occur when the environment of an experiment is so artificial that all who participate are aware that something special is going on and behave uncharacteristically. Such effects constitute a threat to external validity.

Reactive effects of testing—Effects that occur when a premeasure sensitizes participants to the aims of an intervention. Such effects constitute a threat to external validity.

Regression toward the mean—A phenomenon that often occurs upon the second administration of a survey (without any intervention), when respondents who have scored very high or very low on items on the first administration appear to have changed to average scores. Such results, which may be a statistical artifact, are often seen in surveys involving extreme views; such regression constitutes a threat to external validity.

Reliability—The consistency of survey data collected. The data gathered in a survey may be inconsistent if respondents cannot understand or care about the questions or the survey administrator (e.g., interviewer).

Representative sample—A sample in which important population characteristics (e.g., age, gender, health status) are distributed similarly to the way they are distributed in the population at large.

Retrospective designs—Designs for surveys aimed at studying events that have already occurred.

Selection—How people are chosen to participate in a survey and, if the survey study has an experimental design, how participants are assigned to experimental and control groups.

Self-controls—Groups that serve as their own control groups through being surveyed at two different times. Studies using self-controls require premeasures and postmeasures and are called longitudinal, pretest-posttest, or before-after designs.

Solomon four-group design—A study design that combines a randomized control trial with a trial in which some groups receive pre- and postmeasures and some receive only postmeasures.

Survey—A system for collecting information from or about people in order to describe, compare, or explain their knowledge, attitudes, and behavior.

Validity—The accuracy of the information gathered by a survey. A survey is valid if it measures what it purports to. A valid survey instrument is also reliable.

About the Author

Arlene Fink, Ph.D., is Professor of Medicine and Public Health at the University of California, Los Angeles. She is on the Policy Advisory Board of UCLA's Robert Wood Johnson Clinical Scholars Program, a consultant to the UCLA-Neuropsychiatric Institute Health Services Research Center, and President of Arlene Fink Associates, a research and evaluation company. She has conducted surveys and evaluations throughout the United States and abroad and has trained thousands of health professionals, social scientists, and educators in survey research, program evaluation, and outcomes and effectiveness research. Her published works include more than 100 articles, books, and monographs. She is co-author of *How to Conduct Surveys: A Step-by-Step Guide* and author of *Evaluation Fundamentals: Guiding Health Programs, Research, and Policy; Evaluation for Education and Psychology;* and *Conducting Literature Reviews: From Paper to the Internet.*